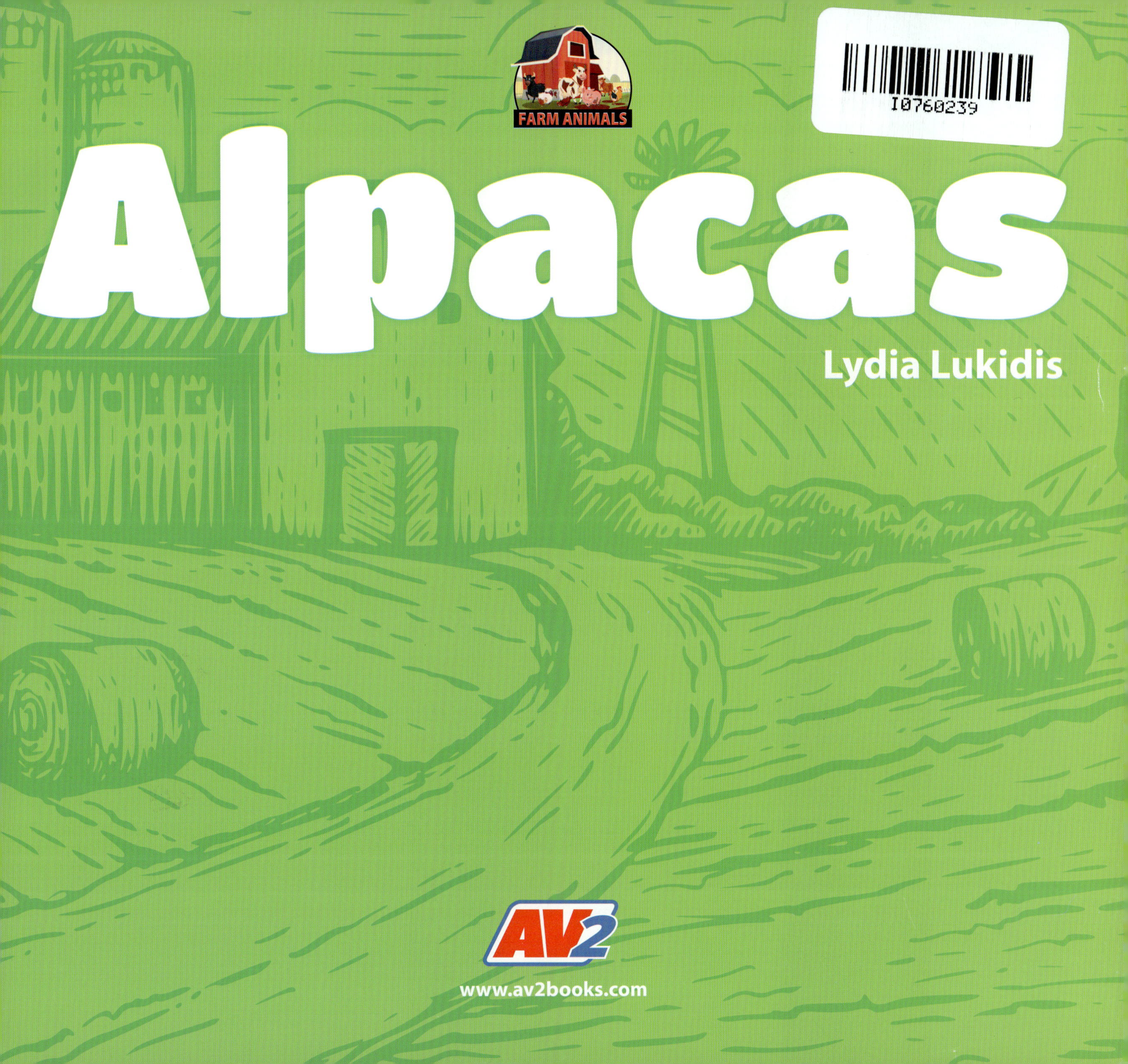


# Alpacas

Lydia Lukidis

AV2

www.av2books.com

**Step 1**
Go to **www.av2books.com**

**Step 2**
Enter this unique code

**WZNIBQ4C2**

**Step 3**
Explore your interactive eBook!

AV2

FARM ANIMALS

Alpacas

Start!

AV2 is optimized for use on any device

## Your interactive eBook comes with...

**Audio**
Listen to the entire book read aloud

**Videos**
Watch informative video clips

**Weblinks**
Gain additional information for research

**Try This!**
Complete activities and hands-on experiments

**Key Words**
Study vocabulary, and complete a matching word activity

**Quizzes**
Test your knowledge

**Slideshows**
View images and captions

**View new titles and product videos at www.av2books.com**

# Alpacas

## Contents

# Alpa

Alpacas are animals that live on a farm.

Farmers raise alpacas for their soft fur coat.

There are **more alpacas** in **Ohio** than **in any** other state.

Alpacas are best known for their long necks.

Long necks help them see far away.

Alpaca fur is called fleece.

It is used to make clothes such as sweaters and jackets.

One alpaca can make up to **10 pounds** of fleece in a year.

Some alpacas have long, curly fleece.

Their fleece looks like hair.

Other alpacas have short, fluffy fleece.

Alpacas do not have top front teeth.

They have lower front teeth that can be more than 1 inch long.

Alpacas often make a soft **humming** noise.

The humming sounds like a cat purring.

Alpacas eat fresh grass.

Sometimes, they eat wood and bark.

Female alpacas have one baby at a time.

A baby alpaca is called a cria.

A newborn alpaca can weigh up to **20 pounds.**

Alpacas do not like to be alone.

They are happiest when they are with other alpacas.

# ALPACA FACTS

These pages provide detailed information that expands on the interesting facts found in the book. They are intended to be used by adults as a learning support to help young readers round out their knowledge of each unique animal featured in the *Farm Animals* series and why it is kept and raised on farms.

**Pages 4–5**

**Alpacas are animals that live on a farm.** Alpacas are native to South America. They were domesticated about 6,000 years ago. People used them for meat and fleece. Today, alpacas live on farms around the world. They were first imported to U.S. farms in the 1980s.

**Pages 6–7**

**Alpacas are best known for their long necks.** Alpacas have thin bodies. Their heads are small with short, pointy ears. Alpacas do not have hooves. They have two toes with toenails. There is a soft pad underneath their feet. When alpacas walk on grass, they do not make footprints.

**Pages 8–9**

**Alpaca fur is called fleece.** Alpaca fleece is very soft. It is also warmer and stronger than sheep wool. Alpaca fleece is water-resistant. It takes longer for it to become wet. Alpacas do not shed their fleece. Farmers usually shave it off once a year.

**Pages 10–11**

**Some alpacas have long, curly fleece.** Alpacas with fluffy fleece are called Huacayas. They make up 90 percent of all alpacas. Alpacas with long hair are called Suris. Their hair needs to be cut often. If not, it will grow long enough to touch the ground.

**Pages 12–13**

**Alpacas do not have top front teeth.** Alpacas have teeth at the back of their mouth to help them chew food. These teeth are called molars. Instead of top front teeth, alpacas have hard gums. The lower front teeth are longer in male Alpacas.

**Pages 14–15**

**Alpacas often make a soft humming noise.** Alpacas are quiet animals. They only make a loud screech if they are scared or angry. When they feel frightened, they may spit, too. Male alpacas can make a deep noise with their throats. They do this to attract female alpacas.

**Pages 16–17**

**Alpacas eat fresh grass.** Alpacas are grazers and mainly feed on grass. Alpacas require less food than most farm animals of their size. They eat about 2 pounds (0.9 kg) of food for every 125 pounds (57 kg) of their body weight. When raised on a farm, they also eat hay.

**Pages 18–19**

**Female alpacas have one baby at a time.** Alpacas usually give birth once a year. They carry their babies for about 11 months. Crias can stand within an hour of being born. They also grow quickly. They reach a weight of more than 100 pounds (45 kg) when they are one year old.

**Pages 20–21**

**Alpacas do not like to be alone.** Alpacas are social animals that like to stay with their herds. It is best for farmers to have more than just one alpaca. Farmers should also provide their alpacas with basic shelter. This protects them from the heat and bad weather.

# KEY WORDS

Research has shown that as much as 65 percent of all written material published in English is made up of 300 words. These 300 words cannot be taught using pictures or learned by sounding them out. They must be recognized by sight. This book contains 50 common sight words to help young readers improve their reading fluency and comprehension. This book also teaches young readers several important content words, such as proper nouns. These words are paired with pictures to aid in learning and improve understanding.

| Page | Sight Words First Appearance |
|---|---|
| 4 | a, animals, are, farm, for, live, of, on, that, their |
| 5 | any, in, more, state, than, there |
| 7 | away, far, help, long, see, them |
| 9 | and, as, can, is, it, make, one, such, to, up, year |
| 10 | have, like, looks, some |
| 12 | do, not |
| 13 | be, they |
| 15 | often, sounds, the |
| 17 | eat, sometimes |
| 18 | at, time |
| 21 | when, with |

| Page | Content Words First Appearance |
|---|---|
| 4 | alpacas, coat, farmers, fur |
| 5 | Ohio |
| 7 | necks |
| 9 | clothes, fleece, jackets, pounds, sweaters |
| 10 | hair |
| 12 | teeth |
| 13 | inches |
| 15 | cat, noise |
| 17 | bark, grass, wood |
| 18 | baby, cria |

Published by AV2
350 5th Avenue, 59th Floor New York, NY 10118
Website: www.av2books.com



Library of Congress Cataloging-in-Publication Data

Names: Lukidis, Lydia, author.
Title: Alpacas / Lydia Lukidis.
Description: New York : AV2 by Weigl, [2019] | Series: Farm animals | Audience: Grades 2-3 | Identifiers: LCCN 2019044573 (print) | LCCN 2019044574 (ebook) | ISBN 9781791116408 (library binding) | ISBN 9781791116415 (paperback) | ISBN 9781791116422 (ebook) | ISBN 9781791116439 (ebook)
Subjects: LCSH: Alpaca--Juvenile literature.
Classification: LCC SF401.A4 L85 2019 (print) | LCC SF401.A4 (ebook) | DDC 599.63/67--dc23
LC record available at https://lccn.loc.gov/2019044573
LC ebook record available at https://lccn.loc.gov/2019044574

Printed in Guangzhou, China
1 2 3 4 5 6 7 8 9 0 24 23 22 21 20

022020
100919

Art Director: Terry Paulhus Project Coordinators: Sara Cucini and Ryan Smith



The publisher acknowledges Shutterstock, Minden, iStock, and Alamy as the primary image suppliers for this title.